POEMS FROM INDIRA

REFLECTIONS
from a Half-Filled
LOOKING GLASS

POEMS FROM INDIRA

REFLECTIONS
from a Half-Filled
LOOKING GLASS

CLIFF RATZA

Poems from Indira
Reflections from a Half-Filled Looking Glass
Copyright © 2021 by **Cliff Ratza**. All rights reserved.

Library of Congress Control Number: 2021951026
ISBN: Paperback: 978-1-7361828-3-3

No part of this publication may be reproduced, stored in a retrieval system or transmitted in any way by any means, electronic, mechanical, photocopy, recording or otherwise without the prior permission of the author except as provided by USA copyright law.

This is a work of fiction. Names, characters, businesses, places, events and incidents are either the products of the author's imagination or used in a fictitious manner. Any resemblance to actual persons, living or dead, or actual events is purely coincidental.

The opinions expressed by the author are not necessarily those of Lightning Brain Press.

Published in the United States of America.

Published by Lightning Brain Press
1. Poetry

Contents

About the Poems: 9
About the Writer: 11
The Conundrum of Time 12
The Bountiful Harvest 13
History's Lesson 14
Tempers Fidget 15
Back to the Future 16
Mother's Day Remembrance 18
Out of Rhythm 19
The Flame of Youth 20
Beyond the Silence 21
For Members Only 22
The Skater 23
The Plainsman's Sonnet 24
Life's Promise 25
The Quiet News 26
Second-Hand Wisdom 27
Amends Remaining 29
Life's Triple Crown 30
Beyond the Pale 31
Rites of Passage 32
Quo Vadis 33
In the Now 34
In the Now – Redux 35
High Tide 36
The Comfort Zone 37

The Arena	38
Dead Reckoning	39
The Atomic Man	40
Bookends	41
Conundrum of the Rather Be's	42
Status Quo Woes	43
Three Turns	44
A Gentler Day	45
Generation Next	46
To Be	47
Lose the Sadness	48
Point of View	49
The Scrivener	50
Winter Portrait	51
The No Shows	53
Momentary Fears	54
Scheherazade	55
Uncertain Joys	56
To the Limit	57
Delicate Blooms of Spring	58
Riddle of the Sphinx	59
Lisa's Garden Party	60
The Far Side	61
The Stranger	62
The Simpler Summer	63
Crossing the Bar	64
Sunday Morn	65
Final Approach	66
Larger than Life	67
Past Imperfect	68
So What So When So Where	69
Silence of the Now	70

Cast Your Fate to the Winds 71
Course Correction.. 72
Wisdom's Reach 73
The Song of the Thrush 74
Singular Season 75
The Graced Land... 76
Post-Second Coming 77
Reach for Beyond 78
The Age of Lesser Men... 79
Carry the Day 80
Sensational Seasons 81
Past Tension 82
Remembrance of Time Future... 83
The Color of Time's Echo 84
The Noble Pair 85
Where Next to Go... 86
Never Let Go 87
Share the Fantasy 88
Don't Fear the Reaper 89

About the Poems:

Readers of "The Lightning Brain Series" know that Electra Kittner and Indira Ramanujan are Kindred Spirits in heart and soul, just as I am Indira's Kindred Spirit in poetry. She is the "Inner Voice" for the poems found in the novels of my first series, and I hope you enjoy them. Those poems are included in my first book of poetry – "Reflections through Life's Hourglass."

My second collection of poems – "Reflections from a Half-Filled Looking Glass" –extends the first by adding new verses conjured from whimsical thoughts gleaned from my "Simple Scholar" view of life and are sprinkled in the books comprising my second series – "The Keepers Series."

I believe that all of us should consider life at least half full; otherwise, it's a tough slog. If you follow this rule, you might find more enjoyment when handling the choices and uncertainties that come your way.

About the Writer:

Cliff Ratza would describe himself as a "Simple Scholar" who enjoys putting into verse his views on the "Human Condition." His poems are written on the run while thoughts occur as he moves through the day. Some are light and whimsical, others more serious. They're written in a modern lyrical or metaphysical style using meter and rhyming schemes that communicate in a clear and engaging manner. He teaches at Chicago area universities, which he combines with business and writing careers. He hopes you find at least some of his poems enjoyable or useful, and he will be pleased if you do.

The Conundrum of Time

Is time real or merely illusion?
Trying to answer will leave you behind.
Ponder no more and spare all confusion,
Take it for granted it's all in your mind.

Time is our relative measuring stick,
That clicks off the process twixt each life event.
When fully engaged there's not even a tick,
No trace or a clue to where the time went.

But when you encounter a trouble or two,
The ticking is loud streaming slowly ahead.
Minutes or seconds stretch way past your view,
The clock's in reverse or perhaps has stopped dead.

Maybe the atoms tell different tale,
Quantum pulse tracking trajectory of time.
But I cannot fathom it's beyond human pale,
So I'll simply believe what is told in this rhyme.

The Bountiful Harvest

The gardener's magic returns every Fall.
Nature's picking and choosing so kind.
Nourishing body but that is not all,
  Find food for the Spirit and Mind.

Gardening teaches that nothing is certain,
It needs time and some effort each day.
Some pluck and some luck help
  draw back Time's curtain,
To show what is coming your way.

It also reveals Life's unerring rhythm.
There's beginning and ending and more.
Spirit's not finite, it's an endless-loop ribbon,
  Forever and ever restored.

So when tending your garden pay
  attention each Season.
Lessons are offered for both Faith and Reason.

History's Lesson

Where are we? I cannot see,
The world's a puzzling place.
And as I'm about to figure things out,
They change at a furious pace.

History's caused by waves of change,
They sweep without set season.
Propelling towards that future shore,
Challenging Faith and Reason.

Yet Life's meant to make the most,
Simply play your part.
History shows time sorts things out,
Each day's a pristine start.

Tempers Fidget

Tempus fugit's a fact of life,
It hurries us through our hectic day.
And when impediments obstruct our path,
Fidgeting tempers will clear the way.

We're built to think both fast and slow,
Each mind-set has its special way.
But when time is ticking too fast to see,
Thinking fast comes into play.

Fast thinking often works so well,
But when to speed's not often clear.
No pat answer to point the way,
Be wary we often prefer high gear.

How to turn the temper down?
Take a deep breath then smile don't frown!

Back to the Future

Not often does my inner eye,
Let old pictures click into view.
Normally its focus set,
On everyday things that I must do.

But then some odd remote emotion,
Intrudes abruptly in my way.
And suddenly an interruption,
Concerns about the elders' day.

I see a Queen who's bent by age,
Majestic spirit standing tall.
I see her kindly king and castle,
He's stepping gently avoiding a fall.

Has the realm beyond wall,
Become a strange foreboding place?
Do they stay within the yard,
And never show an outward face?

My heart transfixed my only wish,
To sweep them into sheltering arms.
Protect them now and evermore,
With magic spells and talisman charms.

Another click the picture shifts,
To a future that is yet to be.
Stunned to see the castle fortress,
My God the walls are there for me!

A final picture snaps for now,
Back to the safety of today.
I must start planning what to do,
But confusion will not go away.

Incipient panic crashes on me,
I'm trapped in living out a lie.
I haven't a clue for what to do.
But pretend that death will pass me by.

Mother's Day Remembrance

You departed abruptly it was unfair.
We all felt numb and cheated.
Nothing to do but sit and stare.
No sad farewells repeated.

Our wishes always to care for you,
For all you gave to us.
Caught off guard you slipped away quickly,
Wanting no bother or fuss.

Gratefully pain free you left on your terms,
Your Beauty and Spirit intact.
You avoided repetition of stories of yore,
Preferring the present not oft looking back.

Our love for you we won't repeat,
The essence you mean or have done.
Instead shine through in all we do,
As we greet each dawning Sun.

Out of Rhythm

Our Life contains a rhythm,
Helping us move along.
Its background beat we're not aware,
We're focused on the song.
But sometimes you might realize,
That the rhythm is all wrong.
And suddenly a quandary,
Just where do you belong?

Nature is quite different,
All creatures know their place.
It seems to be a puzzlement,
Just for the human race.
We're not always in harmony,
Some pieces get misplaced.
But rearrange and thank the stars,
For the gift - a state of grace.

Though we are born of Nature,
We're each a special kind.
Given sense of wonder and awe,
They dance within our mind.
Though part is shared some's separate,
We must search until we find.
That balance in space a singular place,
Reality aligned.

The Flame of Youth

Passions still smolder no matter the year,
Though the fire gets banked over time.
The fever Youth feels from emotions too real,
Becomes a warm glow in your mind.

But passions are tricky they may bring great risk,
You can't simply flee and be free.
Your Fate may have turned so prepare to be burned,
As your hubris is forced to one knee.

Try not to fret for it's not tragedy,
You'll rebalance a life soon enough.
Its not reaching for what might have been right for you,
Never knowing if you had the right stuff.

So you must decide whether young whether old,
To stretch for the stars or let your dream fold.

Beyond the Silence

How clever Man's emergent brain,
Inventing tools to extend his reach.
Gathering knowledge so he can teach,
The outward World is his to gain.

How different the story when looking in,
Enigmas cloud mere mortal mind.
Evidence so hard to find,
What lies beyond the silence within?

Mitered men tell all they know,
Their Faith proclaims what's really there.
But merely sand castles in the Air?
Whither their efforts where do they go?

And so we reach a stalemate,
Faith and Reason to resolve.
Let future worry how to solve,
Enjoy what you have – before too late.

For Members Only

We're each uniquely special,
Yet each must still belong.
To some things larger than ourselves,
It's a blend that makes us strong.

When young we yearn for freedom,
To reach for our morning star.
To explore the world with dreams unfurled,
We're ready to go far.

Yet it's said no man's an island,
So no matter where you roam.
Someday you'll learn you must return,
To safe haven that you call home.

It takes a life of living,
To discover where you belong.
Keep open mind and you will find,
Your instincts won't be wrong.

The Skater

The skimming-sprightly skater on
a brisk-bright winter day,
Detours thin ice and the edges where rough.
Ready to stop when the watch says enough,
Watchful and keeping far out of harm's way.

And like the carefree skater as you
gamely glide through life,
Choose mostly those routes that seem secure,
Avoid or skirt what is unsure,
Dodge whatever may lead to strife.

But one day you might hear the note
that heralds Destiny's call,
And plunge into terrain that to you is uncharted.
No turning back, once you have started,
Heedless of problems or painful pratfall.

So take that chance - don't fear falling through.
Resurface with a new point of view.

The Plainsman's Sonnet

I am what I am I'm a Plainsman,
That's what I have chosen to be.
If Fate were to offer a choice once again,
I'd remain it's the right place for me.

Fame and Fortune beckon to Youth,
To soar to the mountain top live in the Sun.
So they fearlessly bound for that moment of Truth.
No matter the outcome it's what must be done.

They scale the summit and what do they find?
A limitless view for always to please?
Or maybe these heights offer no peace of mind,
So return to your roots where you'll be more at ease.

What's right for you try not to guess,
Keep striving till finding a pinch of success.

Life's Promise

Security and all be right,
Your childhood gave to you.
Making that a singular place,
Your elders saw you through.

The game is new the rules have changed,
Now that you're on your own.
Life's twists and turns and all this earns,
Are yours and yours alone.

Face up to existential state,
To some a horrible curse.
But part of fate is in your hands,
The condition could be worse.

The adult's world offers to you,
No promise for what will be.
Do not retreat just simply greet,
Life's possibility.

The Quiet News

Your good news is just for you,
Not meant for you to share.
The outer world takes a different view,
It's much too busy to care.

Give silent thanks and then move on,
Build on what's bestowed.
Share it like a radiant Sun,
And no returns are owed.

Your character will be revealed,
When Good Fortune turns away.
Stay the course try not to yield,
There comes another day.

Second-Hand Wisdom

(for Youth to consider...)

I must be getting older now,
Thoughts stir in my mind.
They were not here in yesteryear,
It's a sign of age I find.

Life seems so implausible,
The path that brought us here.
The choices made along the way,
Their outcomes were unclear.

But instead of hiding fears within,
Explore them in the light.
Do not give in – don't let them win,
A solution is in sight.

We want to live a life pain-free,
Alas fate's not that way.
Face up to your adversity,
Act now and seize the day.

Search about you for advice,
You'll find a friend or two.
It's up to you so don't think twice,
To find what you should do.

But Wisdom's oft ignored by Youth,
They think it won't apply.
Let them sample Life first-hand,
To learn the lessons why.

Amends Remaining

Sometimes I feel so very sad,
It's taken me so long to see.
The reasons why I struggled so,
When happiness was there for me.

And it's not that I've made a ruin of things,
Much of my past earned passing grade.
But I should have noticed better then,
And lessened the number of errors I made.

I'm sorry I didn't appreciate more,
The people and places and all of the things.
I was too wrapped up in immediacy,
To see a glimmer of what this brings.

But I'm only human with built-in flaws,
Acknowledging this I must move on.
And in time remaining I make a pledge,
To make amends before I'm gone.

Life's Triple Crown

Are you where you want to be?
Engaged in what you want to do?
With those who want to care for you?
Joys of your maturity.

It's not like that past early years,
You search for meaning in your life.
The journey's often fraught with strife,
Some paths may lead to bitter tears.

This crown is worn by very few,
It's oft beyond the outstretched reach.
Try your best but Life will teach,
Be grateful for what's offered you.

Beyond the Pale

We're story-tellers in our soul,
Heralding what the World should be.
Laced with fear and ecstasy,
Perfect paradigms to extol.

But Life is not a scripted play,
Cherished wishes go unfilled.
Castles are so hard to build,
Plans revised by end of day.

Still be inspired by the tale,
Audacious hope for what we thirst,
Reach for the dream you may be first,
You may end up beyond the pale.

Rites of Passage

Each of us is honor-bound,
To act the parts of life we play.
Some aren't fun it will be found,
Can't let your comfort block the way.

Sometimes we're able to choose a role,
More often chance assigns to us.
Some demand a heavy toll,
You can't refuse make little fuss.

Good will follow what you do,
From rites of passage you will grow.
And when your final act is through,
Most of the above you'll finally know.

Quo Vadis

It's true we're always on the move,
A perpetual motion machine.
To and from we wear a groove,
Pause is a short-lived dream.

Often to's a cheerful run,
Preparing to make our mark.
Sometimes from's a half-setting Sun,
An uncertain gathering dark.

Is your quo vadis chosen by you?
Maybe yes or no.
Either way one thing is true,
Keep moving or never know.

In the Now

(Tiana's Poem)

Preparing for the future, is how we spend our days,
Carelessly or with much thought, it's done in many ways.
Or maybe measuring here and now,
compared with where we were,
Either way don't miss today, existence only here.

Good or bad or happy or sad, you
can't escape from now,
No matter how you fret or plead, the Gods will not allow.
So deal with it and make the most,
of what's been dealt to you,
It might require a different look, so reorient your view.

Lose yourself in here and now, and
look for what's at hand,
Use your mind and you will find,
something to make a stand.
An ally in your struggle for whatever comes your way,
To ease your pain or stretch your gain,
act now and seize the day.

In the Now – Redux

(For Electra)

The past is but a memory,
The future a dream unknown.
But your present gives a gift you see,
Opened by you alone.

Past a melancholy view,
No more forever gone.
Future problematic too,
Outcomes may be wrong.

So immerse yourself in what is now,
Engage with what's now here.
Embrace the most that fate allows,
Future memories will be dear.

High Tide

(from Cast Away)

Sometimes I grow weary of maddening fight,
The ticking clock's winning try what I might.
There's danger I know in feeling this way,
But I can't dodge the truth – strength is ebbing away.

So I sit in the stillness at end of the day,
Allow melancholy a moment to stay.
Conjuring images of what used to be,
And for but a moment complain bitterly.

Then extinguish resentment that's burning inside,
Better mood riding on incoming high tide.
Look forward to finding what comes with the Dawn,
There's hope for tomorrow I'm better anon.

The Comfort Zone

Take consolation being old,
By reveling in your comfort zone.
You're past the point of being told,
By surviving long and on your own.

Not so for youth they jump through hoops,
Adults too must toe the mark.
Trained to run in mindless loops,
Or marching madly in the dark.

Lucky those in earlier years,
Who had enough to reach success.
Able to reach beyond their peers,
With neither hitch nor second guess.

But would you trade those struggle-years,
For comfort found in setting Sun?
No you'd never trade those tears,
You want to see your journey done.

And I can't trade the comfort zone,
For hoops and loops to grab brass rings.
My time is past – stand pat alone,
For whatever the pleasant evening brings.

The Arena

Did the arena survived the ring,
Managed to battle to standstill or draw.
Did all I could to plan ahead,
Though most outcomes no one foresaw.

Everyone has time in the ring,
Many will do much better than I.
Steel your emotions and look for an edge,
Give it your best shot you simply must try.

Sooner or later you're on the way out
Chance will decide when the battle is done.
No matter the record you're granted some freedom,
Exchange weathered gloves for a place in the sun.

Unchained from the past so enjoy your today,
And ignore for the nonce what will soon fade away.

Dead Reckoning

I've grieved too long about the past,
Once joys of life have passed away.
Happier times a distant day,
So sad that even love won't last.

But silly me for now I know,
Can't clone emotions that I feel.
Nor conjure the day to make it real,
The world moves on all life is flow.

And love transforms what's deep inside,
Reckon the past no more concerned.
Move forward with the lessons learned,
And bury the past with all that's died.

The Atomic Man

Only atoms and the void,
Wise men figured long ago,
Other views have come full circle,
Contingent evidence will show.

Forged in singular explosion,
In time and space beyond our mind.
Genius probed into beginning,
Faith not Reason left behind.

Mankind has been set adrift,
Free will too a question mark.
Left alone to struggle with,
Conundrums in a deepening dark.

But Mankind designed by chance to thrive,
Whenever black swans swim this way.
Just keep in motion reach for new,
The sun will rise another day.

Bookends

Young and old they think alike,
Calendars will report.
The lens they view their interests through,
The focal point is short.

The future for youth infinity,
Trillions of years away.
Beyond their sight their spirit's light,
They enjoy the now the day.

The days are numbered for the old,
No reason to fret or fear.
Joy is grand for what's near at hand,
The glimmering golden year.

Alas for those wedged in between,
Their focal point is long.
Can't struggle free from adversity,
For future bright and strong.

But no matter what all will endure,
And most will realize.
The place to be is there for free,
It's right before their eyes.

Conundrum of the Rather Be's

How frustrating are the Rather Be's,
Locations or faces you'd prefer to trade places.
How difficult covering all the right bases,
Life is a puzzle being so hard to please.

So what in the world are you going to do?
When young there are people you
trust who might know.
But it takes many moons for the outcomes to show,
So you must be patient and take the long view.

And what do you do when your days number few?
Forget your tomorrows the future is here.
So salute what is present with resolute cheer,
And grab for your gusto let the devil make do!

Status Quo Woes

The status quo I much prefer,
Just being in the groove.
My steps they tread this way before,
They know just how to move.

Alas I'm not adventurous,
Caution's taken hold.
I'm trapped by much uncertainty,
Much effort to be bold.

But fortune favors being bold,
When black swans swim your way.
Transition to a brand-new view,
And thrive another day.

Embrace these words and then move on,
Though doubts won't be completely gone.

Three Turns

Is there something wrong with me?
Excitement's not what used to be.
No problems found that I can see,
But the calendar tells the tale.

Too many years have come and gone,
Things that thrilled have since moved on.
Can't fabricate where I don't belong,
The past is not for sale.

Fate once smiled upon my stars,
Many good things few lasting scars.
Time has come to settle for pars,
No search for a holy grail.

Remember with the changing seasons,
Passions change for singular reasons.

A Gentler Day

Each of us will always have,
Memories with a thrilling feeling.
Suspended time unlimited ceiling,
They are the age-old balming salve.

For each of us the day will come,
Wild joys of life have run their course.
Very few have no remorse,
Tomorrow's passions done and gone.

Now is not to show dismay,
No more for you the sporting life.
What lies ahead has little strife,
Embrace a kind of gentler day.

Generation Next

What's to make of Gener-Next?
They're different from us.
Our parents asked the very same,
We wondered what's the fuss?

The context facing Gener-Next,
Is different from the past.
Built by Generations-Gone,
And morphing what will last.

And so it's been for all the Gens,
Chance deals each a hand.
It's up to you to play things through,
And build your promised land.

For those whose hand has come and gone,
Let Gener-Next reign supreme.
Don't judge by rules made yesterday,
As they stretch to reach their dream.

To Be...

Become your body when exertion is due,
Become your emotions when feelings break through.
Become all your senses when feeling the pain,
Become in the moment again and again.

Become the problem when puzzling through,
Become the solution when knowing what's due.
Become the other when helping the child,
Become what you will when dreams running wild.

No matter the future no outcomes yet told,
So live in the instant and celebrate bold.
Forget all your doubts so you set yourself free,
Unchain your potential for whatever will be.

Lose the Sadness

Sometimes I feel so sad for us,
Our hopes they add up to a fall.
Our history casts a similar pall,
Ashes to ashes dust to dust.

But then I simply must recall,
Think of life as comedy.
Humor-filled not elegy,
We bounce no matter how we fall.

So lose the sadness make it gone,
Life is motion life is flow.
No matter that we come and go,
The phoenix rises from ashes anon.

Point of View

Beware of growing very old,
Obstacles they do abound.
You only want what's safe and sound,
No reason to be bold.

Not so for Youth they seek the thrill,
Striving for what's out of reach.
Lessons that the elders teach,
Never mind the occasional fall.

And so the point of view to take,
Depends upon your current year.
So you decide with conscience clear,
And know what you will make.

The Scrivener

Refer to me as Bartleby,
It fits me to a tee.
I do prefer the not in life,
Deflects some misery.

Others choose to chase their dreams,
Gives purpose so it seems.
Just realize with open eyes,
Beware the doubts the screams.

So you decide which way to go,
You're meant to change and grow,
They form the scrivening of your life,
The outcome time will show.

Winter Portrait

(Chicago's Own)

Wintertime Chicago style,
Slogging through the slush.
10 below a foot of snow,
My 4-wheel drive won't mush.
Slippery streets rock-salted roads,
Commuting is a crush.
Drifts exceeding tire depth,
Must get out and push.

Winter sports are all about,
Skiing 10-foot hill.
Skating in the gale-force cold,
Bound to bring on chill.
Sledding on the rut-filled walks,
Too soon we've had our fill.
Hockey on ice-jagged pond,
Becomes a test of will.

But Chicagoans endure the test,
We're resilient and we're tough.
Old Man Winter we'll stare down,
Until he's had enough.
Relinquishing to splendid Spring,

Pleasant replacing rough.
Upcoming Season displays the reason,
Chi-Town's got right stuff.

The No Shows

Feelings showing embarrassed fright,
Awkward for the subjective me.
My faults and vulnerability,
I try to keep them out of sight.

And what do these emotions add?
Helping navigate the days?
Steering clear of harmful ways?
Nudging me to good from bad?

Alas can't banish from the mind.
Can overpower reason's tune.
Can keep me from disastrous ruin,
This better part of humankind.

Momentary Fears

Do not hurry what's next in store.
Admit your feelings set them free,
Live in your reality,
Seize the day forevermore.

Sometimes it seems so sad to me,
Impossible for me to own.
Can't lock away for me alone,
Can't pause the moment that I see.

I'm a mere point in time and space.
Sharing a path with those most dear,
Together not always but overcome fear,
Give thanks for this present with reverence and grace.

Scheherazade

Have you found Scheherazade?
Voice and tales mesmerize.
Visions dance before your eyes,
Please don't think my question odd.

Found in present or your past?
If so then you will surely know.
That magic spell don't let it go,
Alas for me they all have passed.

Will Scheherazade return to me?
I do not know the place to look.
Directions not on map or book,
May lightning strike and set me free.

Uncertain Joys

The time will come when you will see,
The joys of your uncertainty.
Knowns are ultimately unkind,
Death and taxes come to mind.

Youth of course will disagree,
So much to do contingently.
They yearn to know that all's okay,
When preparing to play another day.

But you will learn to welcome chance,
Gives excitement adds romance.
Gives a purpose to focus on,
Forget long run so soon you're gone.

To the Limit

Your limiting points – did you ever reach?
Exciting and frightening – all wrapped in one.
Ultimately knowing – what can't be done,
Just how do you get there – no one can teach.

Most of us won't journey that way,
Unwilling to handle the tortuous pain.
Unwilling to trade for an uncertain gain,
Declining to trust in whatever might may.

But if you are bold then perhaps you can boast,
You risked to the limit to approach being best.
You dauntlessly fought your most punishing test,
And welcomed the madness of achieving the most.

Delicate Blooms of Spring

How beautiful Youth's fragile bloom.
Lads so strong and spirits high,
Lasses looks for which they'd die,
Perishable so soon they're gone.

Precarious very Life's balancing act.
Juggling pieces a delicate art,
Seeming so often they are coming apart,
Happens so quickly no time to react.

Enchanted love that soon is past.
Joy seeming forever breath taken away,
Hard to imagine one unforeseen day,
No matter how dear but rarely to last.

So much like Spring that joyous season.
Embrace your singular romance,
Rarely found a second chance,
Experience all abandon reason!

Riddle of the Sphinx

(For Leslie and Mike 08/24/2013)

Together you have found a prize,
That singly wouldn't be there.
A conjoint path to future days,
For the life you now will share.

Poets past to current day,
Have tried to unravel love.
Grasping for things to help explain,
What's inside to Gods above.

But it matters not what the Poet says,
Nor what the Pundit thinks,
The essence of love escapes the pen,
It's the Riddle of the Sphinx.

It matters only the two of you,
The thoughts and feelings you share.
Let the World keep spinning merrily,
There is nothing else to compare.

Blessings and Wishes from Family and Friends,
Sun shining today as your journey begins.

Lisa's Garden Party

(Ciao erbacce)

Weeds unsightly creep in nightly,
Sing Hi Ho.
Grow in thickly pull out quickly,
Don't let show.

Hard to kill'em try to chill'em,
Fast they grow.
Only flowers in her bower,
Rainbow-color glow.

But just remember come September,
Soon you'll know.
They'll disappear like hounded deer,
Before the snow.

The Far Side

Think back if you can to a sun-spangled youth.
Gazing serenely at hazy far side,
Ready to plunge in uncertain divide,
Thinking you'll see a revealing truth.

But soon all you learn - paths take many a twist.
Where are you going and where have you been?
Hard to distinguish in great roaring din,
Barely aware of the places you missed.

Perhaps you will see if you reach the far shore.
Some of life's sayings revealed as true,
Which ones for now there is barely a clue,
Don't be presumptuous don't ask for more.

Try not to worry about that far side,
Too soon it approaches - enjoy the brief ride.

The Stranger

Into this world uninvited we're thrown,
Often deceived into thinking we're grand.
Often not knowing the place where we stand,
Nothing provided and nothing we own.

Searching for meaning the myths do abound,
Often promoted by personal cause.
Often ignoring humanity's laws,
Full of such wisdom as word-empty sound.

Remove all the blinders and so understand,
Meaning is found in your singular thought.
Contingently pointing to what might be sought,
But always a stranger in this a strange land.

The Simpler Summer

Simpler Summer once more be returned,
Forgetting nostalgic reverie.
Or people or places that used to be,
Building instead on lessons learned.

No frantic ticking slow pace not spurned,
Mind and body roaming free.
Reaching towards infinity,
An hour be endless each minute reserved.

Dwell in a moment tomorrow be learned,
Take joy in all the near you see.
A second distills eternity,
Till darkly sad ashes one more be interred.

Crossing the Bar

Cross to where you now must be,
Doubt replaced by clarity.
No hindrance bars to set you free,
No whit of worry if others can't see.

How long it took to figure out,
Looking back leaves little doubt.
For chosen path give silent shout,
Resolve provides enforced redoubt.

How long the stay there is no clue,
Bless each morn's sustaining dew.
Till winds of fate blow cold on you,
Announcing what is next to do.

Sunday Morn

Look out on that gloriously cold crystal-
clear snow-jeweled Sunday morn,
Where the excitement of youth not
the certainty of old age is born.
When not a single hair of your golden locks is shorn,
By faraway notes from a tune so forlorn.

Draw in the view drink in the feeling,
Immortality's sighting it sets thoughts a reeling.
And think for the nonce this reality appealing,
Is set there for us with a limitless ceiling.

Glory in living this magic space-time,
Unbridled joy without reason or rhyme.
And never to doubt with a point that's too fine,
This minute this second is yours and is mine.

Final Approach

The glide path can't be seen when young,
The final approach unclear.
Too much left that must be done,
You'll see in later year.

Impatient youth scorns marking time,
Rehearsing is no fun.
Too late they see their fantasy,
Lost hours can't be undone.

So learn this truth before too late,
While gusto awaits your call.
All life is now no rehearsing state,
Let landing cast no pall.

Larger than Life

I admire those persons who grasp for the large,
Banishing doubt and casting life free.
Courageous and bold and willing to charge,
Plenty of Spirit to dream what will be.

Be in the fight that's what you should do,
For then you experience reality.
Not sitting back for a second-row view,
A spectator's eyes haven't keenness to see.

And what about those who do nothing but talk,
Making no effort to think or to do.
Budging not even one step on the walk,
I hope that someday they will pick up a clue.

Past Imperfect

My time for greatness has come and gone,
When mediocre set my bar.
Try as I might I didn't rise far,
I sense I knew this all along.

Pursuing a youth-filled starry dream,
Sometimes we're blinded by the glow.
Refusing to see what others know,
Results confirm a new image to glean.

But perhaps be finally able to say,
The distance gone didn't matter much.
Compared to those you could briefly touch,
It's only a trifle come end of the day.

So What So When So Where

So what if you're told what you should do,
When young great fun make a game of it.
No one gets hurt you see right through,
And learn the art of adjusting the fit.

So when the shorter-shorter days,
Let darkness grow imperceptibly.
You suddenly see there is no maze,
Obscuring the way you're completely free.

So where the double-sided sword,
Cuts indiscriminately both ways.
You wield it without a word,
For whatever the count of remaining days.

Help from others or help from you,
Pick which one when a glimmer comes through.

Silence of the Now

Sullen silence is now what I see,
My once-enchanted world now mute.
My raison d'etre once set now moot,
Must search for bearings now right for me.

All my passions time is scoffing,
An indifferent web is being spun,
I see no joy in the just begun,
No phoenix rising in the offing.

But use all senses take in now here,
Revel in what is just beginning.
Don't compare to losing or winning,
Enjoy what you see and lose the fear.

Cast Your Fate to the Winds

Do you fear spoiling forces now loose on the prowl?
Maybe a feeling you aren't good enough.
Uncertain of handling a life in the rough,
Anxiety causing a permanent scowl.

Or maybe there's fear you'll be hurting too much,
Pleasure and pain are on opposite ends,
The same can be said for your foes and your friends,
But you're only alive when feeling their touch.

So have courage and balance your fears against odds,
Emboldened steps let you cast fate to the winds.
Reach for the prize and ignore others' sins,
Rely on yourself and dismiss the false gods.

Course Correction

Don't labor replacing the greats of the past.
The errand of fools who refusing to see,
That in now-ploughed terrain there's no mystery.
It's a thin-veneer layer that never will last.

Instead strike out boldly for what hasn't been said.
Look outside then in for a coming to be,
Unite reason and passion for a vision you see.
Care not for a judgement it's your word instead.

Long after you're gone there'll be time to decide.
Whether words that you spoke had the power to stay,
Revealing directions that sail away.
And place you with those who will always abide.

Wisdom's Reach

Let your grasp be less than reach,
All through your many years.
For if that's true no fears for you,
It's a lesson life will teach.

Heaven's not your sole reward,
When struggling beyond your dreams.
The battle's worth all that it seems,
Though wounded by the sword.

Indulge in this when old and young,
You're resilient and will survive.
Make the choices so you to thrive,
Let wisdom sing your song.

The Song of the Thrush

My voice has finally come to me,
Like the song of a golden thrush.
I noticed no change till recently,
It emerged an invisible rush.

Like that of the thrush my voice has grown,
On a glidepath never too long.
Distinctive now and standing alone,
To me it's surprisingly strong.

Close to the ground but skylarking on high,
Notes finally rounded and firm.
Whatever they're worth at least I can try,
Giving something of value to learn.

Singular Season

Seasons and years trace hopes and fears,
Shaping your shadow's dim arc.
Giving some joy or sometimes some tears,
Ultimately leading to dark.

Should you try sharing the journey together?
Someone to help with the load?
Perhaps it is better no matter the weather,
If you travel upon the same road.

You must decide for your singular one,
When shadows come into your view.
Remembering always that once it's begun,
Partners can help both pull through.

The Graced Land

May is the glory-filled month of the year.
Green nascence replenishing reticent Earth,
Bursting to pleasure an undisguised mirth,
Giving to all a reality dear.

Gamboling about in ephemeral game.
Primal and pristine and rooted in light,
Not knowing or caring a reckoning night,
Each singular being each year sums the same.

Beauty abounds in a delicate touch.
Empowering purpose in manifest form,
Pregnant desire once more is reborn,
Magic within has no need of a crutch.

Life-giving essence leaves no killing thirst,
Brimming and filling removing decay,
Past is the present no time ticks away,
Bountifully leaving last good as the first.

Look to an order that reaches the deep.
Sit up and take notice no pretenses here,
Subliminally knowing what's meant to be dear,
Controlling and giving whatever's to keep.

Post-Second Coming

The center holds like burnished gold,
Centripetally pulling the knowing.
Sacrifice brought the best of thought,
Life set free and flowing.

One Second Coming has come and gone,
Aberrant against the tide.
Time did prove it baseless and wrong,
Though it posed an addictive side.

But could it come to life once more,
In a sinister form unknown?
The future holds untolds in store,
Slouching towards distant throne.

It's up to all to guard the gate,
Avoid a state of thrall.
Rid all the rough-shod beasts in wait,
Before they come to call.

Reach for Beyond

When young I struggled to reach the truth,
But too short-sighted I could not see.
So I turned to myths and saw forsooth,
The gods they too eluded me.

Then turning to humanity,
I looked for what might be inside.
And using all my empathy,
I found all three they cannot hide.

Let no soul say that truth be told,
One time for all eternity.
Reach for beyond seek out the bold,
And never fear contingency.

The Age of Lesser Men

Each of us is made the same,
From creation in the stars.
Maybe for success or blame,
Approaching the limiting bars.

Alas we dance to tribal tune,
Which changes o'er the years.
Lesser men lead us to ruin,
Unless we handle fears.

Still possible that we can be,
Like greats found in the past.
If our tribal reality,
Becomes better than the last.

Reach beyond self-serving view,
And join the ranks of the great but few.

Carry the Day

Man and Woman are sterner stuff,
Sheltering's out of place.
Shaping by Eons has made us tough,
The entire Human Race.

My empathy goes to those we know,
Who've suffered from Nature's ills.
There's pain and loss but time will show,
We'll win this test of wills.

So stay alert and play your part,
Solidarity is in play.
You have within a lion's heart,
That will surely carry the day.

The Riddle of the Sphinx runs deep,
A treasure meant for you to keep.

Sensational Seasons

Do you see in sunlight falling,
Bare buds on boughs of trees?
Do you sense in breezes calling,
Springtime breaking free?

Every season comes with greetings,
Heralding each and all.
A pristine meaning for your being,
In its alluring call.

So too the seasons of your life,
Awaiting for your mark.
Carve it with your wisdom's knife,
In daylight not in dark.

Celebrate the joys they send,
Savor all before they end.

Past Tension

How do you handle past tension's reflection,
Rippling off what today's in your life?
Don't let it hamper what you're going after,
But consider why it once caused strife.

You've grown far beyond all the troubles of past,
And have bypassed what they once imposed.
To Reality now make sure you hold fast,
Look forward past tense is now closed.

So sit in the Sun on an early Spring day,
And muse at the clouds drifting by.
All the past tension has floated away,
Now distant as blue in the sky.

Remembrance of Time Future

The fullness of Time reveals to me,
What in headier days I failed to see.
Too much for myself not enough for the other,
Too late to reach out but I can't run for cover.

To the Ladies who offered the treasure of feeling,
I would kneel before them my soul set a-reeling.
And to Fellows who helped me by sharing life's load,
Hug but let go before emotions explode.

And to Counselling Elders no more anywhere,
I would offer brave words in one silent prayer.
That I'll work to be worthy of what they gave me,
And trust that a future remembrance will see.

The Color of Time's Echo

I see them still I shan't forget,
The scarf, the tie, the mirth in the eyes.
How simple how easy how fun-filled and yet,
These treasures were offered for me to apprize.

Rich color and pattern bespoke of the grand,
Quick-sounding footsteps brought glorious times.
No sunsetting setbacks were allowed to withstand,
The synchronous rhythm of the clock's cheery chimes.

Alas all has faded except in my mind,
When attraction of memory echoes gently to view.
Long ago feelings reminding and kind,
Point one more time to what shimmers so true.

So wherever the journey of life carries you,
May past reminiscence paint other than blue.

The Noble Pair

We and Nature are but the same,
When scanned at nanoscopic view.
But emergent differences take hold,
When humanity's cachet breaks through.

Personas combine to a singular whole,
Noble yet flawed and partitioned we be.
We try to command but often we fail,
Body Mind and Emotion they total to three.

Always becoming what we're striving for,
Able to grasp only part of the sum.
Then changes sweep in and we're carried away,
Our journey continues towards what will become.

The Golden Philosophers knew this well,
And it's true through time as the calendars tell.

Where Next to Go

Do you know where next to go?
Are you getting primed to leave?
Does your choice provide warm glow?
Did someone point and you believe?

When young pretend you know the place,
This will add to confidence.
And if changing later it's no disgrace,
Consider an act of providence.

Ignore the doubts that linger about,
Until you've stretched far as you dare.
And only then should you turn about,
To find another for which you care.

Never Let Go

Never let emotions go,
When in a singular feeling state.
Let them in and let them flow,
Do it now before too late.

Happy or sad they're telling you,
Something that you now must hear.
All too soon they'll fade from view,
Unknown when they'll again appear.

Hold on tight until you can't,
Pay not a whit to ticking time.
And disappear into their chant,
Feeling every bit of rhyme.

Savor the blend of words and feeling,
That sets your head and heart a-reeling.

Share the Fantasy

Is Life perchance a fantasy,
Conjured merely by lonely thought?
That's half the sum, but more awaits,
When sharing what the others brought.

We often think we know what's right,
When striding in the cheerful day.
But in the doubts of darkening night,
Adjust to what the partners say.

Walking alone is often fast,
But easier to lose your way.
Wait before each die is cast,
Lessen the odds of going astray.

Life is more than just your dream,
Account for serendipity's team.

Don't Fear the Reaper

Death should be of less concern the older we become,
Simply one of Nature's Laws when all our work is done.
Something unavoidable that Life will send our way,
Expected then and brings an end
to day's soft-setting Sun.

For Youth forsooth it's tragedy Death
would come too soon.
Their morning star is still in flight to
reach a bright high noon.
So sad because it cuts them short
with so much yet to say,
Better they should stay awhile and
sing out wine-sweet tune.

For those so close to Mid-Life peak
oh Death is quite unfair,
Much to be accomplished still suspended in the air.
Better for to grant a stay ignore them for awhile,
Returning at a later day when all's been taken care.

But do not fear the Reaper when
becoming gray and old.
For those with faith and hope to see
what's now emerging bold.

Redemption may await for those
on darkling distant isle,
For those who yearn gods grant they
learn as Prophets have foretold.

www.ingramcontent.com/pod-product-compliance
Lightning Source LLC
Chambersburg PA
CBHW030914080526
44589CB00010B/304